LÍNGUA INGLESA

MARIA CRISTINA G. PACHECO
Pesquisadora, licenciada em Pedagogia e Artes Plásticas; docente de língua inglesa e de língua espanhola em diversas instituições de ensino em São Paulo; autora de livros didáticos e paradidáticos em línguas estrangeiras.

MARÍA R. DE PAULA GONZÁLEZ
Docente de língua inglesa e de língua espanhola; coordenadora em vários cursos de idiomas em São Paulo.

5ª edição
São Paulo
2023

Coleção Eu Gosto Mais
Língua Inglesa 3º ano
© IBEP, 2023

Diretor superintendente	Jorge Yunes
Diretora editorial	Célia de Assis
Editores	Isabela Moschkovich e Ricardo Soares
Secretaria editorial e processos	Elza Mizue Hata Fujihara
Assistente de produção gráfica	Marcelo Ribeiro
Ilustrações	Gisele B. Libutti, Lye Kobayashi, Vanessa Alexandre
Projeto gráfico e capa	Aline Benitez
Diagramação	Nany Produções Gráficas

Dados Internacionais de Catalogação na Publicação (CIP) de acordo com ISBD

P116e   Pacheco, Maria Cristina G.

   Eu gosto m@is: Língua Inglesa / Maria Cristina G. Pacheco, Maria R. de Paula González. - 5. ed. - São Paulo : IBEP - Instituto Brasileiro de Edições Pedagógicas, 2023.
   il ; 20,5 cm x 27,5 cm. - (Eu gosto m@is 3º ano)

   Inclui anexo.
   ISBN: 978-65-5696-435-5 (Aluno)
   ISBN: 978-65-5696-436-2 (Professor)

   1. Educação. 2. Ensino fundamental. 3. Livro didático. 4. Língua inglesa. I. González, Maria R. de Paula. II. Título. III. Série.

2023-1174   CDD 372.07
                                                 CDU 372.4

Elaborado por Odilio Hilario Moreira Junior - CRB-8/9949

Índice para catálogo sistemático:
1. Educação - Ensino fundamental: Livro didático 372.07
2. Educação - Ensino fundamental: Livro didático 372.4

5ª edição – São Paulo – 2023
Todos os direitos reservados

Rua Gomes de Carvalho, 1306, 11º andar, Vila Olímpia
São Paulo – SP – 04547-005 – Brasil – Tel.: (11) 2799-7799
www.editoraibep.com.br   editoras@ibep-nacional.com.br
Impresso na Leograf Gráfica e Editora - Julho/2023.

APRESENTAÇÃO

Querido aluno, querida aluna,

Elaboramos para vocês a **Coleção Eu gosto m@is**, rica em conteúdos e atividades interessantes, para acompanhá-los em seu aprendizado.

Desejamos muito que cada lição e cada atividade possam fazer vocês ampliarem seus conhecimentos e suas habilidades nessa fase de desenvolvimento da vida escolar.

Por meio do conhecimento, podemos contribuir para a construção de uma sociedade mais justa e fraterna: esse é o nosso objetivo ao elaborar esta coleção.

Um grande abraço,

As autoras

SUMÁRIO

LESSON

1 A house or an apartment? 6
(Casa ou apartamento?)
- **Communicative contents:** talking about houses and apartments
- **Grammar content:** adjectives; opposites; verb to live

2 I'm hungry! 16
(Estou com fome!)
- **Communicative contents:** buying at the supermarket
- **Grammar content:** verbs to like and to love.

3 Meals 28
(Refeições)
- **Communicative contents:** talking about meals; numbers
- **Grammar content:** verbs to have and there is / there are; prepositions

4 Is there a supermarket near here? 36
(Há um supermercado aqui perto?)
- **Communicative contents:** going shopping; locations; days of the week
- **Grammar content:** adverbs; verbs to go, to play and to swim

5 I like jeans 48
(Eu gosto de *jeans*)
- **Communicative contents:** talking about clothes and shoes; sizes; colors; seasons of the year and months
- **Grammar content:** verbs to like, to need and to color

LESSON

6   Are you ready to order?.. 60
(Você já quer fazer o pedido?)
- Communicative contents: talking about meals, eating at restaurants
- Grammar content: verb to order; How much…?

7   I don't feel very well 70
(Eu não me sinto muito bem)
- Communicative contents: talking about health and diseases
- Grammar content: verbs to ache, to feel, to look well/sick, auxiliary should

8   What did everybody do last weekend? 82
(O que todo mundo fez no último fim de semana?)
- Communicative contents: talking about the weekend
- Grammar content: past tense of verbs

GLOSSARY 94
(Glossário)

COMPLEMENTARY ACTIVITIES 97
(Atividades complementares)

LESSON 1

A HOUSE OR AN APARTMENT?
(Casa ou apartamento?)

This is
a big house.

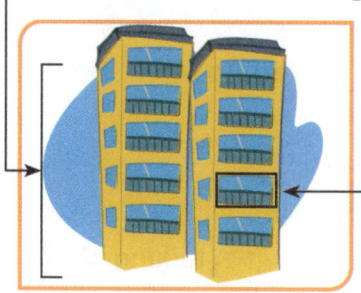

This is a building.

This is
an apartment.

This is
a small house.

Listen and read.
(Escute e leia.)

I live in an apartment. And you?

Me too.

Do you live in a house or in an apartment?

I live in an apartment.

Do you live in a house or in an apartment?

I live in a house.

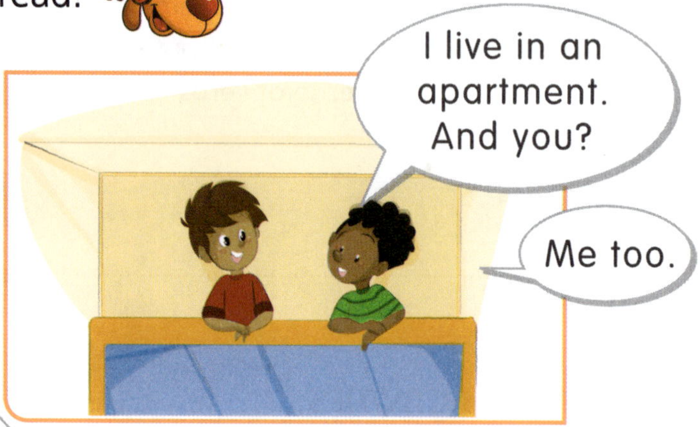

ACTIVITIES

1 **Where do you live?**
(Onde você mora?)

I live in _____.

2 Listen to the dialogue and check (✓) the correct option.
(Escute o diálogo e marque a opção correta.)

a) Is your house comfortable?
- ☐ Yes, it is.
- ☐ No, it is not.

b) Is your house big?
- ☐ Yes, it is.
- ☐ No, it is not.

c) Is your apartment small?
- ☐ Yes, it is.
- ☐ No, it is not.

d) Is your apartment old?
- ☐ Yes, it is.
- ☐ No, it is not.

e) Is your house new?
- ☐ Yes, it is.
- ☐ No, it is not.

f) Is your apartment modern?
- ☐ Yes, it is.
- ☐ No, it is not.

g) Is your house bright?
- ☐ Yes, it is.
- ☐ No, it is not.

h) Is your house ugly?
- ☐ Yes, it is.
- ☐ No, it is not.

VOCABULARY

beautiful: lindo(a).
big: grande.
bright: claro(a).
comfortable: confortável.
dark: escuro(a).
modern: moderno(a).
new: novo(a).
old: velho(a)/antigo(a).
small: pequeno(a).
ugly: feio(a).

3 Write.
(Escreva.)

> **Examples:**
>
> 1. – Is your house **modern**?
>   (Sua casa é moderna?)
>   – No, my house is **old**.
>   (Não, minha casa é antiga.)
>
> 2. – Is your house **big**?
>   (Sua casa é grande?)
>   – No, my house is **small**.
>   (Não, minha casa é pequena.)

a) – Is your house _____? (big/small)

– No, my house is _____.

b) – Is your house _____? (old/new)

– No, my house is _____.

c) – Is your house _____? (beautiful/ugly)

– No, my house is _____.

d) – Is your apartment _____? (dark/bright)

– No, my apartment is _____.

e) – Is your apartment _____? (modern/old)

– No, my apartment is _____.

Attention!
(Atenção!)

big ≠ small
modern ≠ old
beautiful ≠ ugly

old ≠ new
dark ≠ bright

9

4 Let's write.
(Vamos escrever.)

Example:
This house has one **kitchen**.
(Esta casa tem uma cozinha.)
This house doesn't have a **dining room**.
(Esta casa não tem sala de jantar.)

a) This house has one _____.

b) This house has one _____.

c) This house has three _____.

d) This house doesn't have a _____.

5 Unscramble the words and match to the pictures.
(Desembaralhe as palavras e ligue-as às imagens.)

NEKICTH

MOBATHOR

NINIDG OROM

GVLINI ORMO

ROBEDOM

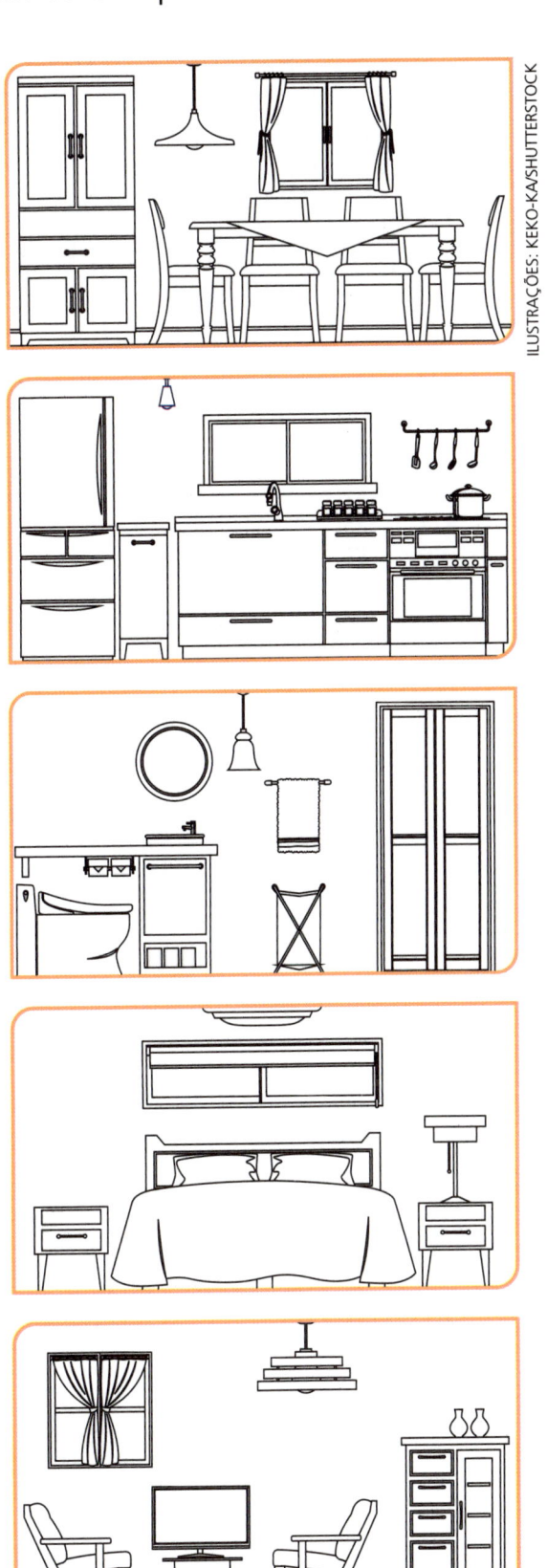

6 Let's write.
(Vamos escrever.)

Example:
– Is this bedroom big?
(Este quarto é grande?)
– Yes, this bedroom is **big**.
(Sim, este quarto é grande.)
or
(ou)
– No, this bedroom is **not big**. It is small.
(Não, este quarto não é grande. Ele é pequeno.)

a) – Is this kitchen modern?

– Yes, this kitchen

is _____.

b) – Is this living room comfortable?

– Yes, this living room

is _____.

c) – Is this bathroom old?

– No, this bathroom

is not _____.

It is _____.

d) – Is this dining room dark?

– No, this dining room

is not _____.

It is _____.

12

7 Check (✓) the correct alternative.
(Marque a alternativa correta.)

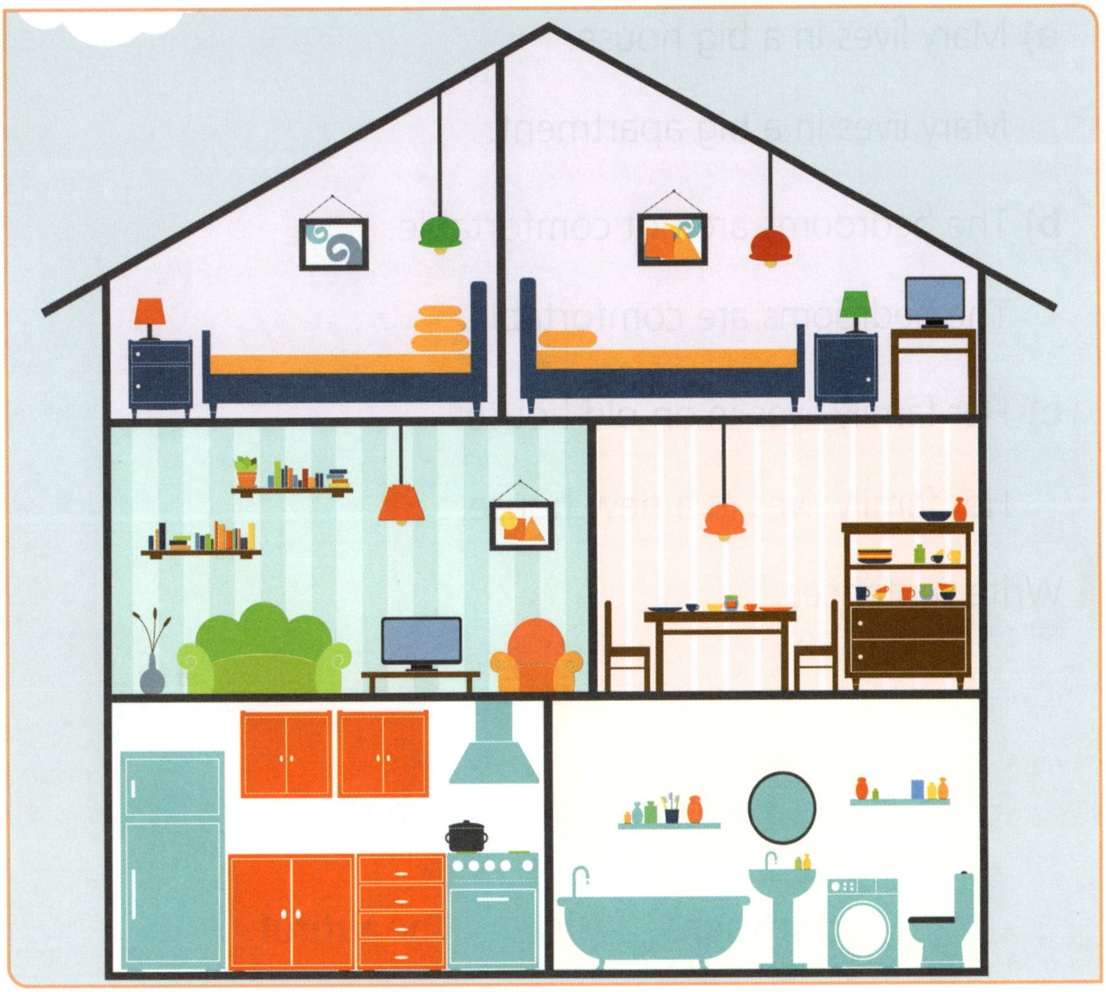

a) ☐ Two bedrooms.   ☐ Three bedrooms.

b) ☐ Two kitchens.   ☐ One kitchen.

c) ☐ Two bathrooms.   ☐ One bathroom.

d) ☐ One living room and one dining room.   ☐ Two living rooms.

8 Listen and circle.
(Escute e circule.)

a) Mary lives in a big house.

   Mary lives in a big apartment.

b) The bedrooms are not comfortable.

   The bedrooms are comfortable.

c) Her family lives in an old house.

   Her family lives in a new house.

9 Write sentences.
(Escreva frases.)

in

live   My   you

apartment   in   beautiful

house   house   live   is

Do   a   an   I

a) _____ live in a _____.

b) Do _____ in an _____?

c) My _____ is _____.

14

10 Let's write.
(Vamos escrever.)

a) My teacher lives in _____ house.

(an old | a new)

b) My grandmother lives in _____ house.

(a beautiful | an ugly)

c) My friend lives in _____ house.

(a modern | an old)

d) I live in _____ house.

(a bright | a dark)

11 Let's play Architect. Look at the blueprint and go to page 99.
(Vamos brincar de arquiteto. Veja a planta de um apartamento e vá até a página 99.)

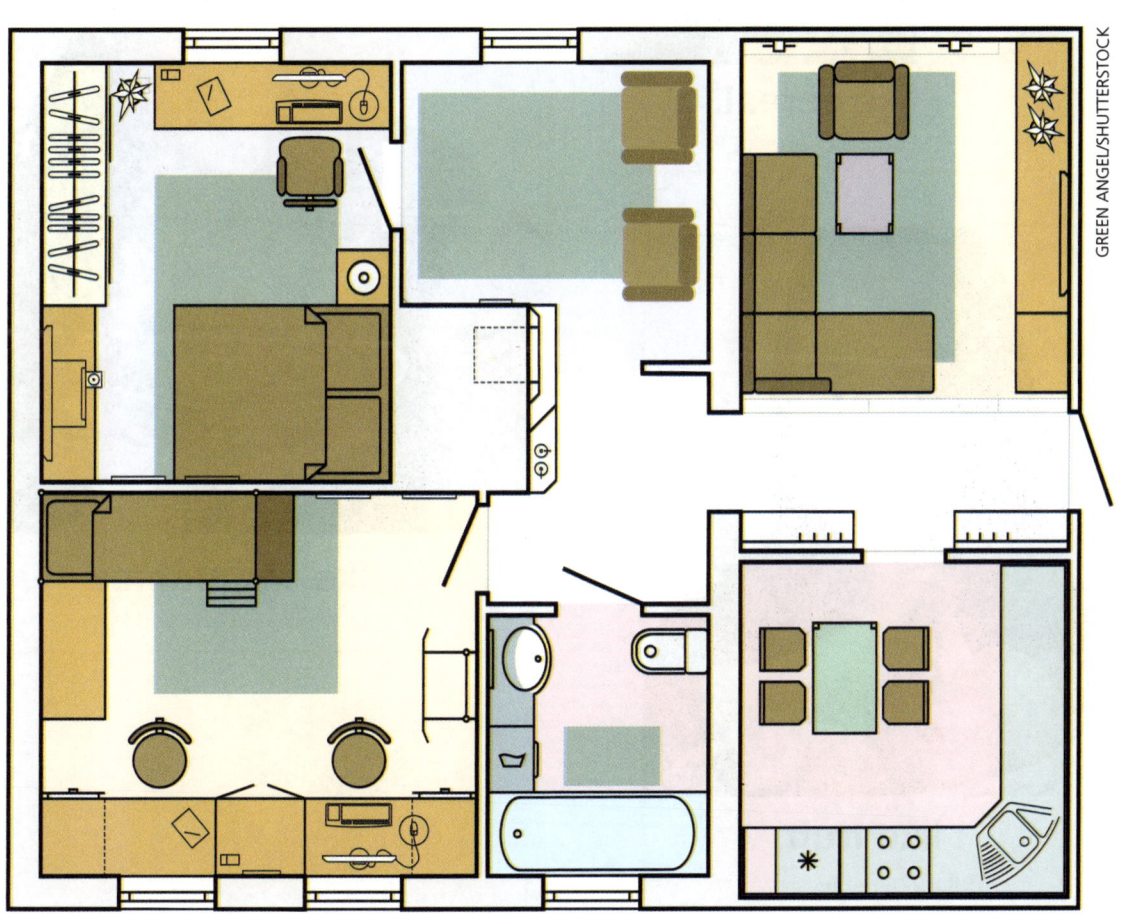

I'M HUNGRY!
(Estou com fome!)

Listen and read.
(Escute e leia.)

I like cereal.
(Eu gosto de cereais.)

I like vegetables.
(Eu gosto de legumes e verduras.)

I like fruit.
(Eu gosto de frutas.)

16

FRUITS
(Frutas)

bananas
(bananas)

pineapples
(abacaxis)

pears
(peras)

lemons
(limões)

apples
(maçãs)

oranges
(laranjas)

ACTIVITIES

1 Let's talk and write.
(Vamos falar e escrever.)

lemons bananas apples oranges

Example:
She likes **pears**.
(Ela gosta de peras.)

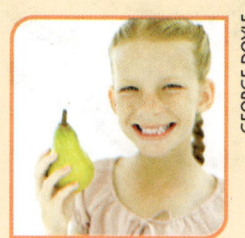

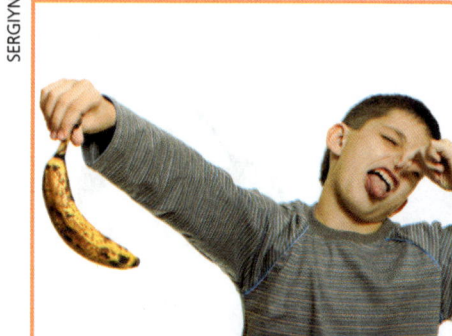

GEORGE DOYLE

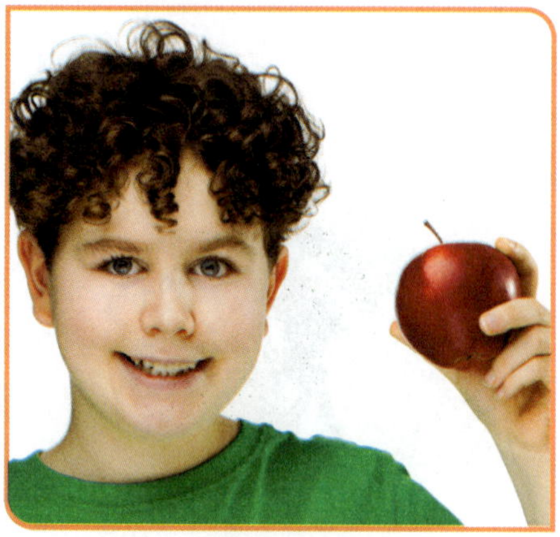
JACEK CHABRASZEWSKI

a) He likes ____________.

SERGIYN

c) He doesn't like ____________.

DAVID HERNANDEZ

b) He doesn't like ____________.

S-F/SHUTTERSTOCK

d) He likes ____________.

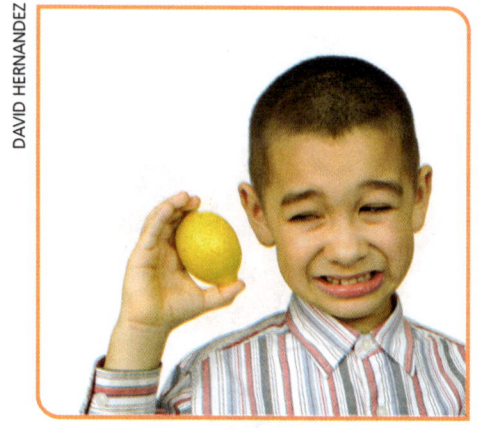

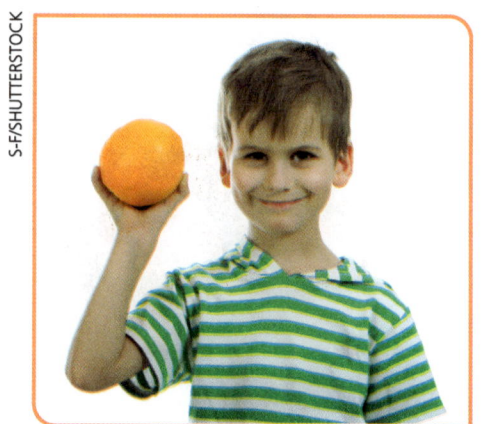

VEGETABLES
(Verduras e legumes)

lettuce
(alface)

broccoli
(brócolis)

potatoes
(batatas)

onions
(cebolas)

pumpkin
(abóbora)

spinach
(espinafre)

cauliflower
(couve-flor)

carrots
(cenouras)

2 Let's talk and write.
(Vamos falar e escrever.)

spinach   potatoes   carrot   pumpkin

Example:
He likes **tomatoes**.
(Ele gosta de tomates.)

a) She likes _____.

c) He likes _____.

b) He doesn't like _____.

d) She doesn't like _____.

CEREALS, PASTA AND DRINKS
(Cereais, massas e bebidas)

pasta
(macarrão)

rice
(arroz)

corn flakes
(cereais de flocos de milho)

bread
(pães)

tea
(chá)

coffee
(café)

juice
(suco)

milk
(leite)

21

3 Let's talk and write.

(Vamos falar e escrever.)

pasta   bread   milk   juice

Example:
I like **corn flakes**.
(Eu gosto de cereais de flocos de milho.)

STOCKBYTE

JACEK CHABRASZEWSKI

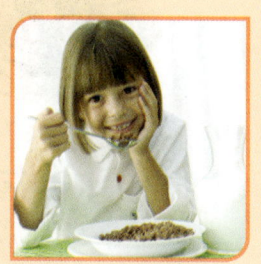

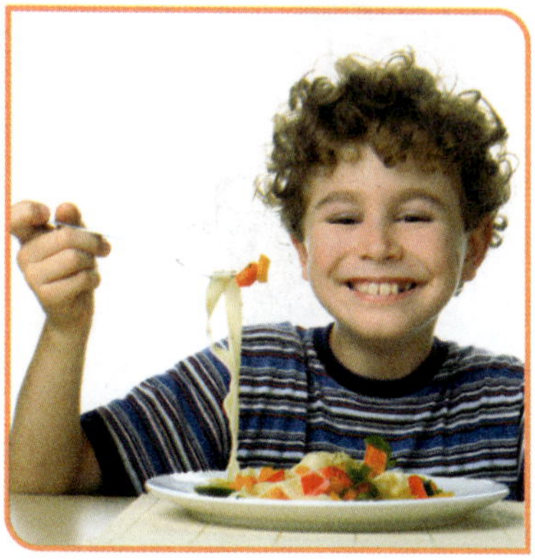

MICHAL KOWALSKI/SHUTTERSTOCK

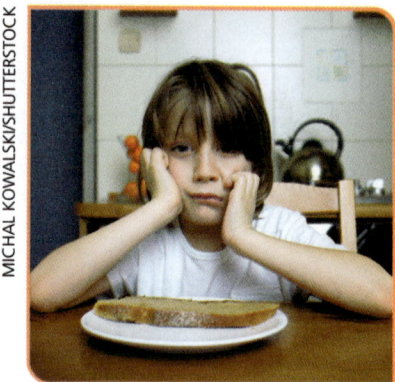

a) He likes ________________.

c) I don't like ________________.

LARISA LOFITSKAYA

PEDALIST/SHUTTERSTOCK

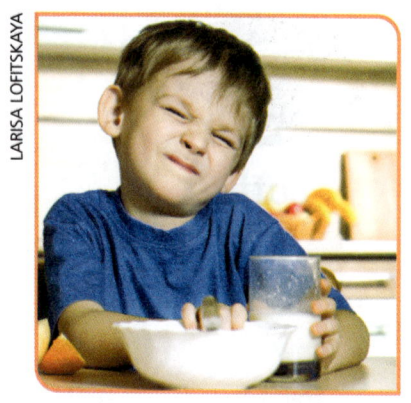

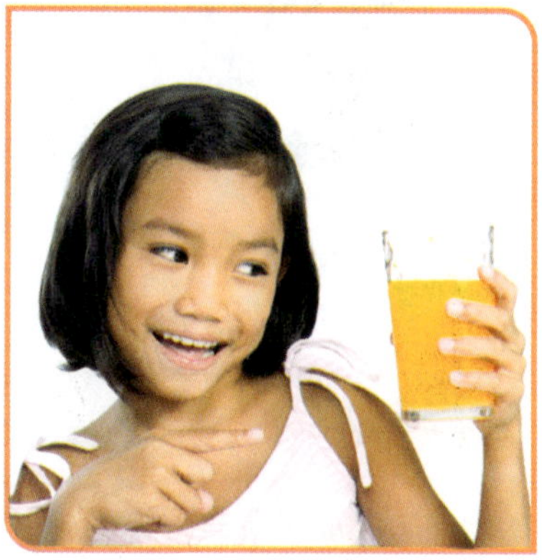

b) I don't like ________________.

d) She likes ________________.

4 Let´s play the Memory Game and make sentences! Go to page 101.

(Vamos jogar o Jogo da Memória e formar frases! Vá para a página 101.)

AT THE SUPERMARKET
(No supermercado)

5 Let's listen and write a supermarket list.
(Vamos escutar e escrever uma lista de supermercado.)

Example:

List

1 kilogram of sugar

½ kilogram of coffee

2 cartons of milk

1 package of crackers

1 box of chocolate

List

_____
_____
_____
_____
_____

 **Attention!**
(Atenção!)

kilogram
(quilo)

box
(caixa)

carton
(caixa do tipo longa vida)

½ kilogram
(meio quilo)

package
(pacote)

23

6 Let's match.
(Vamos ligar.)

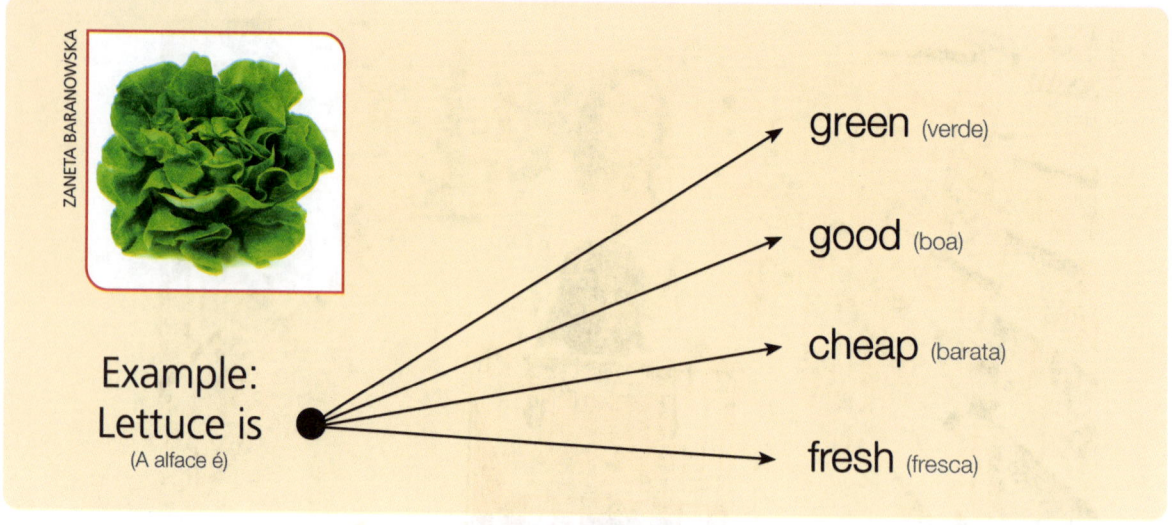

Example:
Lettuce is
(A alface é)

→ green (verde)

→ good (boa)

→ cheap (barata)

→ fresh (fresca)

green
(verde)

red
(vermelho/a)

brown
(marrom)

white
(branco/a)

good
(bom/boa)

bad
(ruim)

apples

oranges

potatoes

milk

fresh
(fresco/a)

old
(velho/a)

sweet
(doce)

orange
(laranja)

cheap
(barato/a)

expensive
(caro/a)

24

7 Write the characteristics. Use the adjectives you have learned before.
(Escreva as características. Use os adjetivos que você aprendeu anteriormente.)

8 Let's play Food Domino. Go to page 103.
(Vamos jogar dominó. Vá para a página 103.)

25

REVIEW
(Revisão)

I can describe a house or an apartment.				
(Eu sei descrever uma casa ou um apartamento.)			
• big	• beautiful	• old	• bright
• new	• dark	• comfortable	
• modern	• small	• ugly	

1 Answer.
(Responda.)

a) Do you live in a house or in an apartment?

I live in _____.

b) Is your house big or small?

My house is _____.

c) Is your house new or old?

My house is _____.

2 Match the opposites.
(Relacione os opostos.)

a) big

b) modern

c) beautiful

d) old

e) dark

☐ ugly

☐ new

☐ small

☐ bright

☐ old

26

I can name these fruits and vegetables, cereals, pasta and drinks.
(Eu sei os nomes de algumas frutas, verduras e legumes, cereais, massas e bebidas.)

Fruit	Vegetables	Cereals, pasta and drinks
• apple • banana • orange • pear • pineapple • lemon	• potato • onion • lettuce • cauliflower • broccoli • carrot • spinach • pumpkin	• bread • corn flakes • rice • tea • coffee • juice • milk

3 Write four sentences. Use the names of the fruits you know.
(Escreva quatro frases. Use os nomes das frutas que você conhece.)

a) _____

b) _____

c) _____

d) _____

4 Write four sentences. Use the names of the vegetables you know.
(Escreva quatro frases. Use os nomes de verduras e legumes que você conhece.)

a) _____

b) _____

c) _____

d) _____

LESSON 3

MEALS
(Refeições)

What do you usually have for...
(O que vocês normalmente comem no...)

breakfast
(café da manhã)

- juice (suco)
- milk (leite)
- bread (pão)
- butter/margarine (manteiga/margarina)
- jam (geleia)

lunch
(almoço)

- rice and beans (arroz e feijão)
- potatoes (batatas)
- steak (bife)
- meat (carne)

dinner
(jantar)

- soup (sopa)
- grilled chicken (frango grelhado)
- salad (salada)

snacks
(lanches)

- sandwich (sanduíche)
- cookies (biscoitos)
- fruit salad (salada de frutas)
- ice cream (sorvete)
- cake (bolo)

28

ACTIVITIES

1 Let's talk and write.
(Vamos falar e escrever.)

bread
(pão)

ice cream
(sorvete)

chicken
(frango)

rice and beans
(arroz e feijão)

cake
(bolo)

fruit salad
(salada de frutas)

pears
(peras)

soup
(sopa)

milk
(leite)

a) I usually have _____

_____ for breakfast.

b) I have _____

_____ for lunch.

c) I have _____

_____ for dinner.

d) I have _____

_____ for snacks.

29

2 **Complete according to the pictures.**
(Complete de acordo com a figura.)

a) Mary likes _____
   for breakfast.

b) Lisa likes _____
   for lunch.

c) I like _____
   for dinner.

d) I like _____
   for snack.

e) She likes _____
   for lunch.

3 Let's draw a delicious meal. Write what you eat.
(Vamos desenhar uma refeição deliciosa. Escreva o que você come.)

4 Who is a vegetarian?
(Quem é vegetariano?)

Vegetarians are people who don't eat any meat, and sometimes dairy or eggs. They eat lots of vegetables, fruit and different kinds of cereal.

There are many kinds of vegetarians. Here are some of them:
- Lacto-ovo vegetarian: doesn't eat meat, but eats eggs and dairy (milk, butter, cheese).
- Ovo-vegetarian: doesn't eat meat or dairy products, but eats eggs.
- Vegan: doesn't eat meat, any dairy products or eggs.
- Some people are semi-vegetarian. They usually eat foods made from plants, and sometimes eat eggs, dairy, fish or poultry.

Answer the questions.

a) What foods do vegetarian people eat?

_____

b) Match.

lacto-ovo vegetarian	•	•	no meat
		•	no animal products
ovo-vegetarian	•	•	dairy (milk, butter, cheese)
		•	eggs
vegan	•	•	no meat or dairy products

c) Are you a vegetarian? Why or why not?

_____

_____

MORE NUMBERS
(Mais números)

11 Eleven	12 Twelve	13 Thirteen	14 Fourteen	15 Fifteen
16 Sixteen	17 Seventeen	18 Eighteen	19 Nineteen	20 Twenty
21 Twenty-one	22 Twenty-two	23 Twenty-three	24 Twenty-four	25 Twenty-five
26 Twenty-six	27 Twenty-seven	28 Twenty-eight	29 Twenty-nine	30 Thirty
31 Thirty-one	32 Thirty-two	33 Thirty-three	34 Thirty-four	35 Thirty-five
36 Thirty-six	37 Thirty-seven	38 Thirty-eight	39 Thirty-nine	40 Forty
41 Forty-one	42 Forty-two	43 Forty-three	44 Forty-four	45 Forty-five
46 Forty-six	47 Forty-seven	48 Forty-eight	49 Forty-nine	50 Fifty

5 Complete the numbers. Go to pages 105 and 107.
(Complete com os números. Vá para as páginas 105 e 107.)

6 Let's play bingo with numbers. Go to page 109.
(Vamos escutar e jogar bingo com os números. Vá para a página 109.)

THERE IS / THERE ARE
(Há)

There is an apple on the plate.
(Há uma maçã no prato.)

There are three apples on the plate.
(Há três maçãs no prato.)

There are two onions and some potatoes here.
(Há duas cebolas e algumas batatas aqui.)

There are some bananas in the bowl.
(Há algumas bananas na tigela.)

7 Let's cut. Go to pages 111 and 113.
(Vamos recortar. Vá para as páginas 111 e 113.)

8 Let's answer.
(Vamos responder.)

Example:
– Is there milk on the table?
– Yes, **there is**.

a) – Is there an orange on the plate?

– Yes, _____.

b) – Are there potatoes in the bowl?

– No, _____.

c) – Is there juice in the fridge?

– Yes, _____.

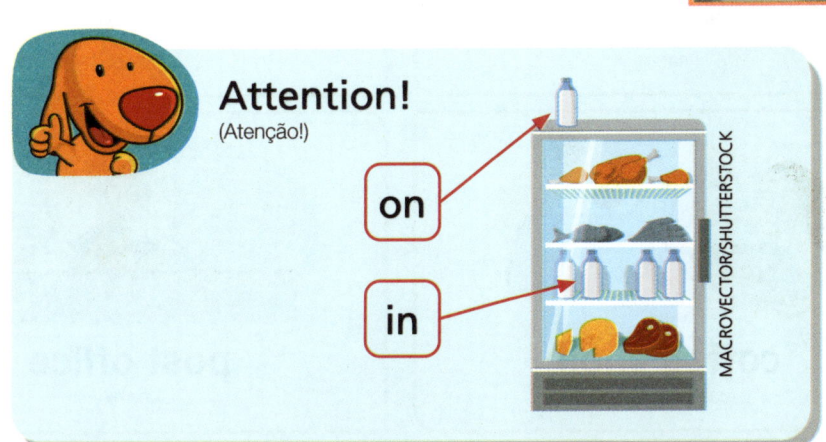

Attention!
(Atenção!)

on

in

35

LESSON 4

IS THERE A SUPERMARKET NEAR HERE?
(Há um supermercado aqui perto?)

Listen and read.
(Escute e leia.)

supermarket
(supermercado)

drugstore
(farmácia)

bookstore
(livraria)

restaurant
(restaurante)

theater
(teatro)

bank
(banco)

coffee shop
(cafeteria, café)

post office
(correio)

ILUSTRAÇÕES: VANESSA ALEXANDRE

36

ACTIVITIES

1 Complete.
(Complete.)

There is a _____ near here.

There are a _____ and a _____ near my school.

There isn't a _____ near school.

There aren't a _____ near here.

There isn't a _____ near my house.

2 Answer the questions.
(Responda às perguntas.)

a) – Is there a supermarket near here?

– Yes, _____.

b) – Are there a school and a drugstore near here?

– No, _____.

c) – Is there a theater near your house?

– No, _____.

d) – Is there a restaurant near school?

– No, _____.

e) – Is there a drugstore here?

– Yes, _____.

37

3 My neighborhood.
(Minha vizinhança.)

Examples:
The school is **near** the hospital.
(A escola está próxima ao hospital.)
The restaurant is **next** to the bank.
(O restaurante está ao lado do banco.)

a) The supermarket is _____ the post office.

b) The coffee shop is _____ to the supermarket.

c) The bank is _____ to the restaurant.

d) The drugstore is _____ the post office.

e) The bank is _____ the school.

f) The bookstore is _____ to the coffe shop.

4) Draw and write.
(Desenhe e escreva.)

restaurant   school   houses   drugstore
post office   supermarket   coffee shop   hospital

_____
_____

Example:
There is a supermarket **near** my house.
(Há um supermercado perto da minha casa.)

a) There is _____ to my house.

b) There is _____ my house.

c) There are _____ house.

d) There is _____.

5 Let's find the places.
(Vamos encontrar os lugares.)

S	U	P	E	R	M	A	R	K	E	T	R	M
C	V	Z	E	U	P	Z	N	L	O	V	T	B
O	M	N	X	O	D	K	V	B	V	F	H	O
F	O	N	A	B	A	N	K	S	G	B	E	O
F	N	P	I	J	T	T	C	H	M	S	A	K
E	G	Q	H	I	B	O	U	R	I	D	T	S
E	R	E	S	T	A	U	R	A	N	T	E	T
S	I	G	F	X	E	T	V	J	Q	C	R	O
H	R	D	R	U	G	S	T	O	R	E	X	R
O	F	C	Q	R	K	D	P	K	M	J	Z	E
P	O	S	T	O	F	F	I	C	E	A	I	F

Write the words that you found.
(Escreva as palavras que você encontrou.)

_____   _____

_____   _____

_____   _____

_____   _____

THE DAYS OF THE WEEK
(Os dias da semana)

JANUARY					
Monday (segunda-feira)	1	8	15	22	29
Tuesday (terça-feira)	2	9	16	23	30
Wednesday (quarta-feira)	3	10	17	24	31
Thursday (quinta-feira)	4	11	18	25	
Friday (sexta-feira)	5	12	19	26	
Saturday (sábado)	6	13	20	27	
Sunday (domingo)	7	14	21	28	

6 What day is it today?

Today is _____.

Attention!
(Atenção!)

On Monday
(Na segunda)

On Tuesday
(Na terça)

On Wednesday
(Na quarta)

On Thursday
(Na quinta)

On Friday
(Na sexta)

On Saturday
(No sábado)

On Sunday
(No domingo)

DAILY ACTIVITIES
(Atividades diárias)

On Mondays and Wednesdays, they go to the library.
(Às segundas e quartas, eles vão à biblioteca.)

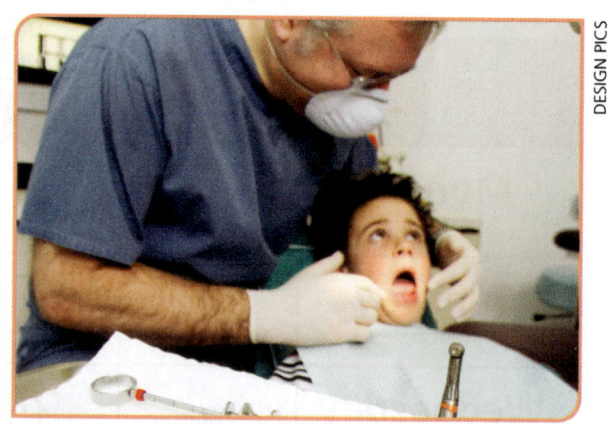

On Tuesdays, Mark goes to the orthodontist.
(Às terças, Mark vai ao ortodontista.)

On Thursdays, I swim at the club.
(Às quintas, eu nado no clube.)

On Fridays, she plays tennis.
(Às sextas, ela joga tênis.)

On Saturdays, we go to a restaurant.
(Aos sábados, nós vamos a um restaurante.)

On Sundays, I play soccer with my friends.
(Aos domingos, eu jogo futebol com meus amigos.)

7 Read the text.
(Leia o texto.)

My name is Mary and I live in Salvador, Bahia. My house is near Lacerda Elevator.

I go to school in the morning. It's near my house.

My best friends are Kevin and Lucy. I usually play soccer with Kevin on Fridays and I swim with Lucy on Saturdays.

On Tuesdays, my brother Carlos and I go to the club to play voleyball. He usually plays on Fridays as well.

On Sundays, we visit our grandparents or sometimes we go to the beach.

Check (✓) the correct sentences.
(Assinale as frases corretas.)

a) Mary lives in Salvador.

b) She has four friends.

c) On Fridays, she plays soccer.

d) On Sundays, she sometimes goes to the beach.

43

8 Let's listen, write and match.
(Vamos escutar, escrever e ligar.)

Monday

Tuesday

Wednesday

Thursday

Friday

Saturday

Sunday

9 What about your week? Go to pages 115 e 117.
(E a sua semana? Vá para as páginas 115 e 117.)

44

10 Survey. Interview your friends.
(Enquete. Entreviste seus amigos.)

a) What time do you go to school?

☐ morning ☐ afternoon ☐ night

b) What time do you have dinner?

☐ afternoon ☐ evening ☐ night

c) What is your favorite vegetable?

☐ lettuce ☐ potato ☐ spinach

d) What is your favorite sport?

☐ soccer ☐ volleyball ☐ cycling

e) Do you live in a house or in an apartment?

☐ house ☐ apartment

f) What is your favorite color?

☐ blue ☐ red ☐ green

REVIEW
(Revisão)

I can talk about the meals in a day.
(Eu sei falar sobre as refeições do dia.)

• breakfast	• lunch	• dinner	• snacks

1 Match the columns.
(Ligue as colunas.)

a) breakfast ☐ cookies

b) lunch ☐ bread

c) dinner ☐ steak

d) snacks ☐ grilled chicken

I can count to 50.
(Eu sei contar até 50.)

11 eleven	17 seventeen	30 thirty
12 twelve	18 eighteen	40 forty
14 fourteen	19 nineteen	42 forty-two
15 fifteen	20 twenty	50 fifty

2 Write the numbers.
(Escreva os números.)

a) 13 _____

b) 16 _____

c) 28 _____

d) 35 _____

I can name these locations.		
(Eu sei nomear estes locais.)		
• supermarket	• school	• coffee shop
• bank	• drugstore	• bookstore
• hospital	• restaurant	• post office

3 Answer the questions.
(Responda às perguntas.)

> Use: *Yes, there is.* or *No, there isn't.*

a) Is there a supermarket near your house?
_____

b) Is there a bookstore near here?
_____

I can name the days of the week.			
(Eu sei nomear os dias da semana.)			
• Sunday	• Tuesday	• Thursday	• Saturday
• Monday	• Wednesday	• Friday	

4 Unscramble the words.
(Desembaralhe as palavras.)

YDASTUAR

[ ]

TYUAEDS

[ ]

YDADENEWS

[ ]

YDAFIR

[ ]

47

LESSON 5

I LIKE JEANS
(Eu gosto de *jeans*)

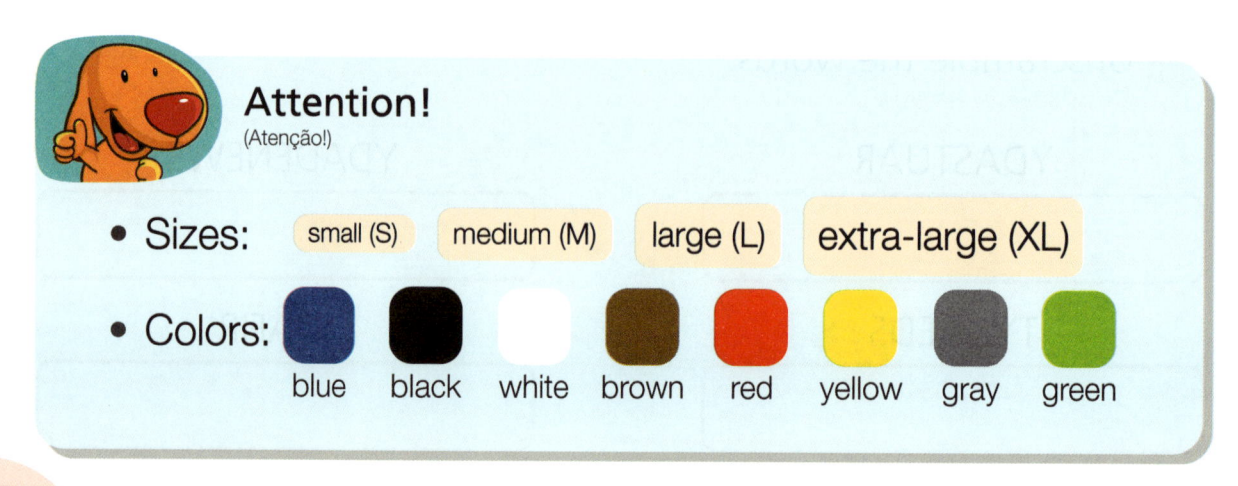

Listen and read.
(Escute e leia.)

- earrings
- cap
- necklace
- T-shirt
- bracelet
- jacket
- jeans (pants)
- dress
- belt
- socks
- sandals
- tennis shoes

Attention!
(Atenção!)

- **Sizes:** small (S) medium (M) large (L) extra-large (XL)
- **Colors:** blue black white brown red yellow gray green

48

ACTIVITIES

1 Show how you like to dress. Draw or glue a picture.
(Mostre como você gosta de se vestir. Desenhe ou cole uma figura.)

VOCABULARY

belt: cinto.
blouse: blusa.
bracelet: pulseira.
cap: boné.
dress: vestido.
earrings: brincos.
extra-large: extragrande.
jacket: jaqueta.
jeans (pants): calça *jeans*.
large: grande.

medium: médio(a).
necklace: colar.
pants: calças.
sandals: sandálias.
shoes: sapatos.
skirt: saia.
small: pequeno(a).
socks: meias.
T-shirt: camiseta.
tennis shoes: tênis.

49

2 Let's color.
(Vamos colorir.)

a) Choose your favorite piece of clothing and check (✓).
(Escolha a sua peça de roupa favorita e marque.)

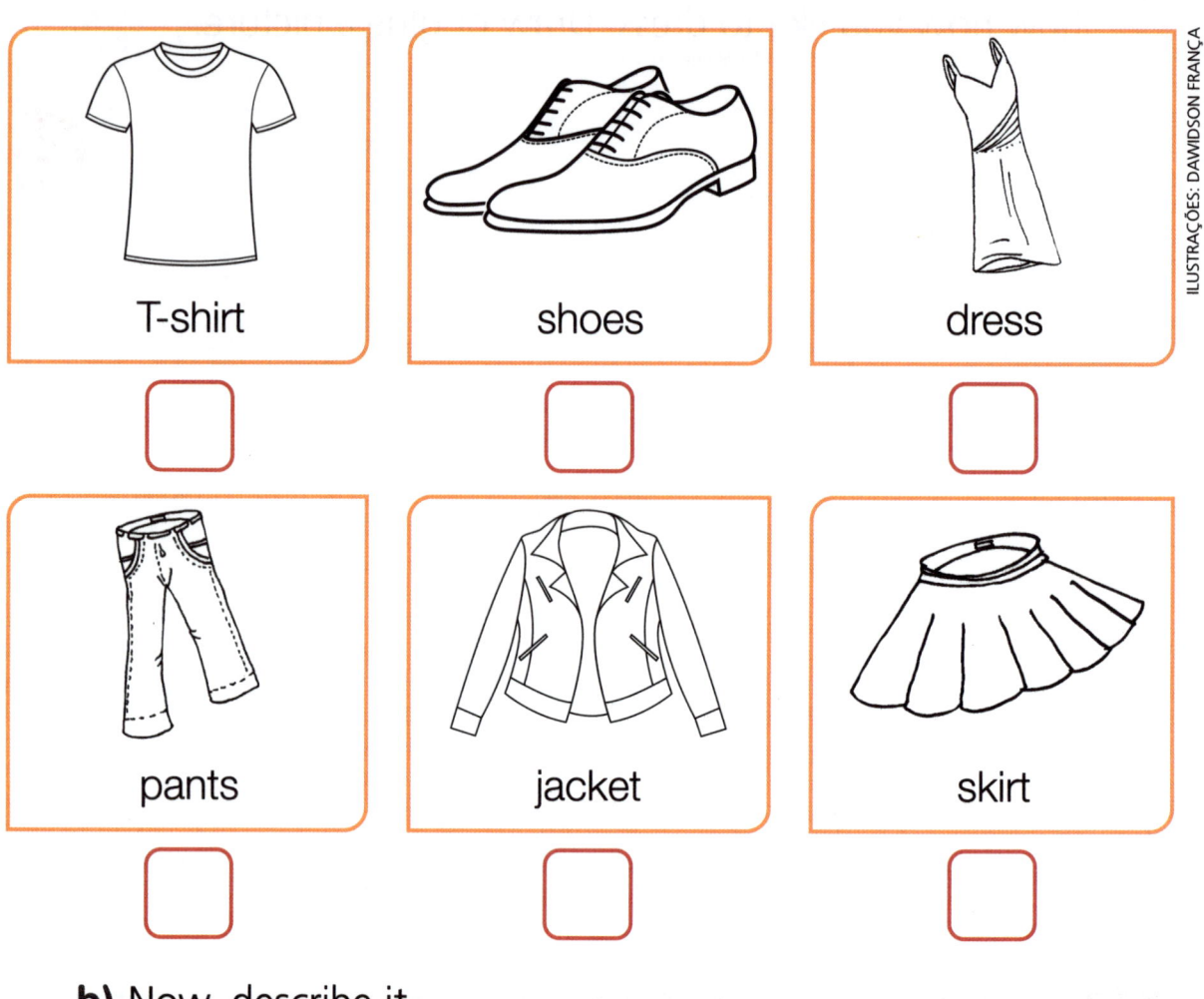

T-shirt	shoes	dress
☐	☐	☐

pants	jacket	skirt
☐	☐	☐

b) Now, describe it.
(Agora, descreva-a.)

> Example:
> My favorite piece of clothing is a **skirt**.
> It's **blue**.

My favorite piece of clothing is _____.

It's _____.

3 Let's write.
(Vamos escrever.)

| skirt | jacket | dress |
| T-shirt | shoes | pants |

Example:

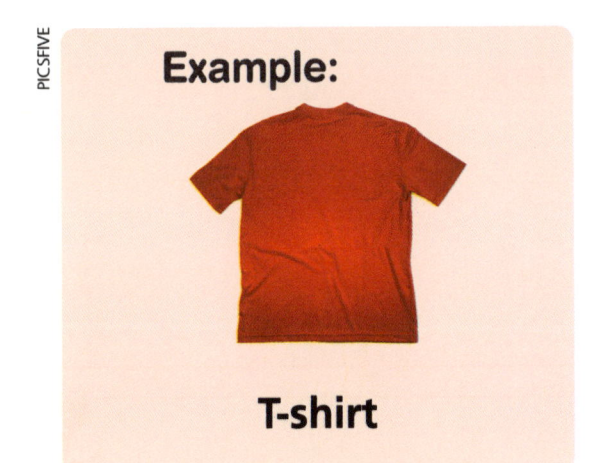

T-shirt

4 Let's cut and glue. Go to page 119.
(Vamos recortar e colar. Vá para a página 119.)

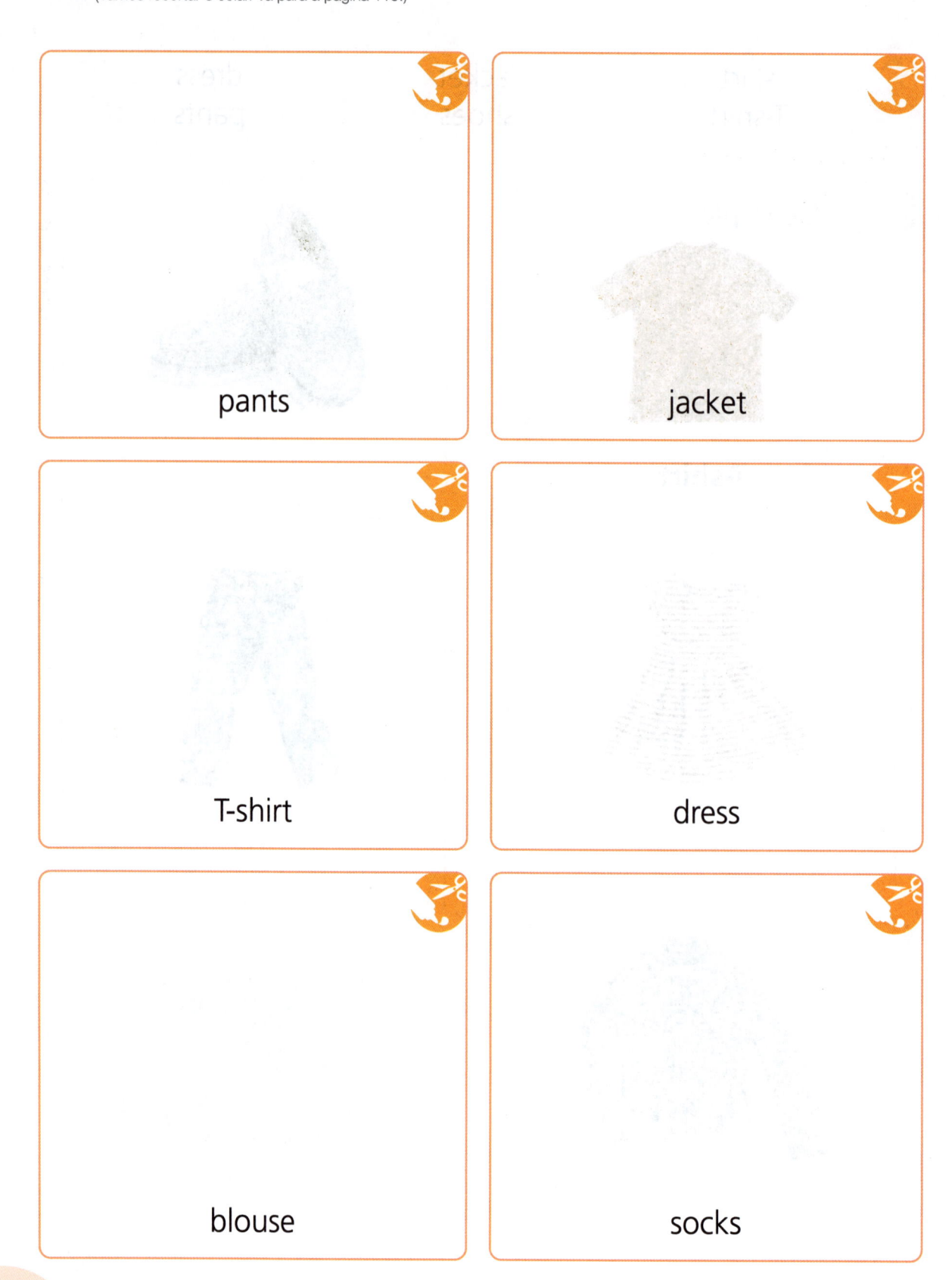

pants	jacket
T-shirt	dress
blouse	socks

SEASONS OF THE YEAR
(Estações do ano)

Summer
(verão)

Winter
(inverno)

Spring
(primavera)

Fall
(outono)

5 Let's match.
(Vamos ligar.)

Example:

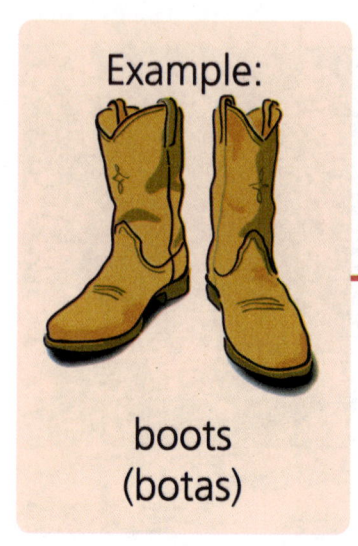

boots
(botas)

sweater
(agasalho)

bikini
(biquíni)

Winter

Spring

Summer

Fall

sandals
(sandálias)

shorts
(bermudas)

scarf
(cachecol)

54

MONTHS OF THE YEAR
(Meses do ano)

JANUARY						
SUN	MON	TUE	WED	THU	FRI	SAT
					1	2
3	4	5	6	7	8	9
10	11	12	13	14	15	16
17	18	19	20	21	22	23
24/31	25	26	27	28	29	30

FEBRUARY						
SUN	MON	TUE	WED	THU	FRI	SAT
	1	2	3	4	5	6
7	8	9	10	11	12	13
14	15	16	17	18	19	20
21	22	23	24	25	26	27
28						

MARCH						
SUN	MON	TUE	WED	THU	FRI	SAT
	1	2	3	4	5	6
7	8	9	10	11	12	13
14	15	16	17	18	19	20
21	22	23	24	25	26	27
28	29	30	31			

APRIL						
SUN	MON	TUE	WED	THU	FRI	SAT
				1	2	3
4	5	6	7	8	9	10
11	12	13	14	15	16	17
18	19	20	21	22	23	24
25	26	27	28	29	30	

MAY						
SUN	MON	TUE	WED	THU	FRI	SAT
						1
2	3	4	5	6	7	8
9	10	11	12	13	14	15
16	17	18	19	20	21	22
23/30	24/31	25	26	27	28	29

JUNE						
SUN	MON	TUE	WED	THU	FRI	SAT
		1	2	3	4	5
6	7	8	9	10	11	12
13	14	15	16	17	18	19
20	21	22	23	24	25	26
27	28	29	30			

JULY						
SUN	MON	TUE	WED	THU	FRI	SAT
				1	2	3
4	5	6	7	8	9	10
11	12	13	14	15	16	17
18	19	20	21	22	23	24
25	26	27	28	29	30	31

AUGUST						
SUN	MON	TUE	WED	THU	FRI	SAT
1	2	3	4	5	6	7
8	9	10	11	12	13	14
15	16	17	18	19	20	21
22	23	24	25	26	27	28
29	30	31				

SEPTEMBER						
SUN	MON	TUE	WED	THU	FRI	SAT
			1	2	3	4
5	6	7	8	9	10	11
12	13	14	15	16	17	18
19	20	21	22	23	24	25
26	27	28	29	30		

OCTOBER						
SUN	MON	TUE	WED	THU	FRI	SAT
					1	2
3	4	5	6	7	8	9
10	11	12	13	14	15	16
17	18	19	20	21	22	23
24/31	25	26	27	28	29	30

NOVEMBER						
SUN	MON	TUE	WED	THU	FRI	SAT
	1	2	3	4	5	6
7	8	9	10	11	12	13
14	15	16	17	18	19	20
21	22	23	24	25	26	27
28	29	30				

DECEMBER						
SUN	MON	TUE	WED	THU	FRI	SAT
			1	2	3	4
5	6	7	8	9	10	11
12	13	14	15	16	17	18
19	20	21	22	23	24	25
26	27	28	29	30	31	

6 Let's write.
(Vamos escrever.)

- September, October and November
- December, January and February
- June, July and August
- March, April and May

a) In Brazil, Summer is

in _____

and _____.

b) In Brazil, Fall is

in _____

and _____.

c) In Brazil, Winter is

in _____

and _____.

d) In Brazil, Spring is

in _____

and _____.

7 Write the sentences below the pictures.
(Escreva as frases embaixo das imagens.)

- I go to the beach in January.
- Our vacation is in July.
- In Brazil, Winter is in June, July and August.
- My birthday is on February 9th.
- Mother's Day is in May.
- In the USA, Winter is in December, January and February.

8 Listen and check (✓) the correct alternatives.
(Escute e marque as alternativas corretas.)

a) Carnival is...

☐ in August.

☐ in February or March.

b) Mother's Day is...

☐ in October.

☐ in May.

c) Father's Day is...

☐ in August.

☐ in January.

d) Children's Day is...

☐ in October.

☐ in July.

e) Christmas is...

☐ in March.

☐ in December.

f) Black Awareness Day is...

☐ in November.

☐ in December.

g) Brazil's Independence Day is...

☐ in August.

☐ in September.

h) International Worker's Day is...

☐ in May.

☐ in June.

9 Think and answer.
(Pense e responda.)

> Example:
> My birthday is in **February**.
> (Meu aniversário é em Fevereiro.)

a) When is your birthday?
(Quando é seu aniversário?)

My birthday is in _____.

b) When is your vacation?
(Quando são suas férias?)

My vacation is in _____.

c) When is Carnival?
(Quando é o Carnaval?)

Carnival is in _____.

d) When is Christmas?
(Quando é o Natal?)

Christmas is in _____.

10 Let's copy and match.
(Vamos copiar e ligar.)

Summer _____   Outono

Winter _____   Verão

Spring _____   Inverno

Fall _____   Primavera

LESSON 6

ARE YOU READY TO ORDER?
(Você já quer fazer o pedido?)

Listen and read.
(Escute e leia.)

Are you ready to order?

Can I have a hamburger and French fries?

Yes. Can I have a salad with lettuce and tomatoes?

VOCABULARY

apple pie: torta de maçã.
cake: bolo.
cheese: queijo.
chicken: frango.
fish: peixe.
French fries: batata frita.
hot dog: cachorro-quente.
ice cream: sorvete.
juice: suco.

meat: carne.
potato: batata.
rice and beans: arroz e feijão.
salad: salada.
sandwich: sanduíche.
soda: refrigerante.
soup: sopa.
tomato: tomate.
water: água.

ACTIVITIES

1 Check (✓) to form groups.

desserts

| chocolate cake ☐ | soup ☐ | fruit salad ☐ | apple pie ☐ |

drinks

| juice ☐ | soda ☐ | salad ☐ | water ☐ |

lunch and dinner

| salad ☐ | fish ☐ | ice cream ☐ | rice and beans ☐ |

fast food

| hamburger ☐ | rice and beans ☐ | hot dog ☐ | French fries ☐ |

61

2 What would you like to eat? Complete.
(O que você gostaria de comer? Complete.)

| salad | soup | French fries | hamburger |
| tomatoes | orange | juice | chocolate cake |

Example:
– Are you ready to order?
– Yes. Can I have a **hamburger** and **French fries**, please?
– Yes, you can.

a) Can I have _____ and _____, please?

b) Can I have _____ and _____, please?

3 Let's practice and write.
(Vamos praticar e escrever.)

Example:
– What is your order for lunch?
– Can I have a **tomato salad**?

a) – What is your order for dinner?

– Can I have _____?

b) – What is your dessert order?

– Can I have _____?

c) – What is your lunch order?

– Can I have _____?

4 Let's match!
(Vamos relacionar!)

a) chicken

b) meat

c) fish

d) soup

e) juice

f) salad

g) cake

h) French fries

i) hamburger

j) potatoes

5 Let's talk and write.
(Vamos conversar e escrever.)

> chicken   salad   sandwich
> fish   cheese   soda
> potato   soup   hamburger
> meat   juice
> cake   French fries

a) My three favorite foods:

My favorite foods are _____

_____.

b) My favorite drink:

My favorite drink is _____

_____.

c) My favorite dessert:

My favorite dessert is _____

_____.

d) Write things a friend likes:

My friend likes _____

_____.

e) Write things your father likes:

My father likes _____

_____.

6 Make your menu. Go to page 121.
(Faça seu cardápio. Vá para a página 121.)

7 Are you hungry? Let's make something tasty!
(Você está com fome? Vamos fazer algo gostoso!)

Burger

- Sesame seed bun (top)
- Cheese
- Tomato
- Burger
- Lettuce
- Middle bun
- Cheese
- Tomato
- Burger
- Bun

Fruit salad

- Banana
- Strawberry
- Grape
- Orange
- Pineapple
- Mint

65

8 How much is it?
(Quanto é?)

Examples:
– How much is it?
– It is R$ 15,00.
– OK. Thanks.

EMILIA STASIAK

VOCABULARY

How much? Quanto?
Thanks: obrigado(a).
You're welcome: de nada.

a) – _____ is the ice cream?

– It is _____.

– Thanks.

– OK.

RMNOA357/SHUTTERSTOCK

b) – How much are the French fries?

– They're _____.

– _____.

– OK.

ALAN BAILEY/SHUTTERSTOCK

c) – _____ is the meat?

– It's _____.

– Thanks.

– _____.

BESTPHOTOSTUDIO/SHUTTERSTOCK

Now, use the menu on page 123.

9 Let's listen, draw and write.
(Vamos escutar, desenhar e escrever.)

REVIEW
(Revisão)

I can name these clothes.		
\(Eu sei nomear estas roupas.\)		
• cap	• jeans	• pants
• T-shirt	• dress	• socks

1 Match.
(Relacione.)

a) cap   ☐ camiseta

b) socks   ☐ boné

c) dress   ☐ meias

d) T-shirt   ☐ vestido

I can name the seasons of the year.			
(Eu sei os nomes das estações do ano.)			
• Summer	• Spring	• Winter	• Fall

2 Match.
(Ligue.)

a) Summer   Primavera

b) Fall   Inverno

c) Spring   Verão

d) Winter   Outono

I can talk about the months of the year.			
(Eu sei falar sobre os meses do ano.)			
• January	• April	• July	• October
• February	• May	• August	• November
• March	• June	• September	• December

3 Complete.
(Complete.)

a) Write the month of your birthday.

My birthday is in _____.

b) Write the month when we celebrate Mother's Day.

Mother's Day is in _____.

I can order at a restaurant and say my favorite foods and drinks.
(Eu sei fazer um pedido em um restaurante e falar minhas comidas e bebidas favoritas.)
— Are you ready to order? — Yes. Can I have some orange juice, please? — Coming right up!

4 Complete with the right word.
(Complete com a palavra correta.)

a) What is your order?

Can I have a _____, please?

b) What about your drink?

Can I have _____, please?

some water
salad

69

LESSON 7

I DON'T FEEL VERY WELL
(Eu não me sinto muito bem)

Listen and read.
(Escute e leia.)

What's the matter?

I don't feel very well.

headache
(dor de cabeça)

sore throat
(dor de garganta)

fever
(febre)

earache
(dor de ouvido)

cold
(resfriado)

cough
(tosse)

toothache
(dor de dente)

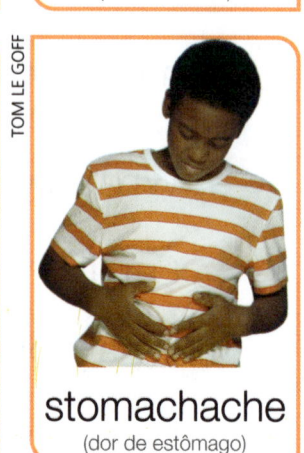

stomachache
(dor de estômago)

ACTIVITIES

1 Let's write. Use the words from the box.
(Vamos escrever. Use as palavras do boxe a seguir.)

> headache   fever   toothache   earache

a) Lucy doesn't feel very well.

She has a _____.

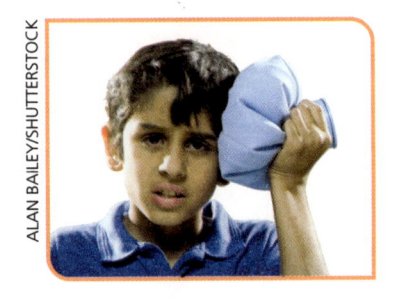

b) John doesn't feel very well.

He has a _____.

c) Allan doesn't feel very well.

He has a _____.

d) Caroline doesn't feel very well.

She has an _____.

2 Listen and read the following text.
(Escute e leia o texto a seguir.)

Lisa: — Hi, Rita! Good morning! You don't look good.

Rita: — Hi, Lisa! I don't feel very well.

Lisa: — What is the matter?

Rita: — I have a headache and a terrible sore throat.

Lisa: — Oh, that's too bad. Maybe you should see a doctor.

Rita: — Yes, I think that's a good idea.

3 Check the sentences as true (T) or false (F).
(Assinale se as frases são verdadeiras ou falsas.)

a) Rita doesn't look good.

☐ T   ☐ F

b) Rita has a stomachache and a headache.

☐ T   ☐ F

c) Rita has a headache and a sore throat.

☐ T   ☐ F

d) Rita should see a doctor.

☐ T   ☐ F

4 Be careful with the yellow fever.
(Cuidado com a febre amarela.)

YELLOW FEVER

Early symptoms of yellow fever include

Sudden onset of fever

Chills

Severe headache

Back pain

General body aches

Nausea and vomiting

Fatigue and weakness

Severe cases include

High fever

Bleeding and shock

Yellow discoloration of the skin and the whites of the eyes

73

5 Let's answer.
(Vamos responder.)

Example:

What's the matter, Peter?

I don't feel very well. I have a stomachache.

a) What's wrong, Mary?

I don't feel very well.

_____

_____. **(cough)**

b) What's the matter, Paul?

I don't feel very well.

_____

_____. **(fever)**

c) What's wrong, Jim?

I don't feel very well.

_____

_____. **(cold)**

d) What's the matter, Sarah?

I don't feel very well.

_____

_____. **(toothache)**

e) What's wrong, Mom?

I don't feel very well.

_____

_____. **(headache)**

f) What's the matter, Dad?

I don't feel very well.

_____

_____. **(sore throat)**

LET'S GO TO THE DENTIST!
(Vamos ao dentista!)

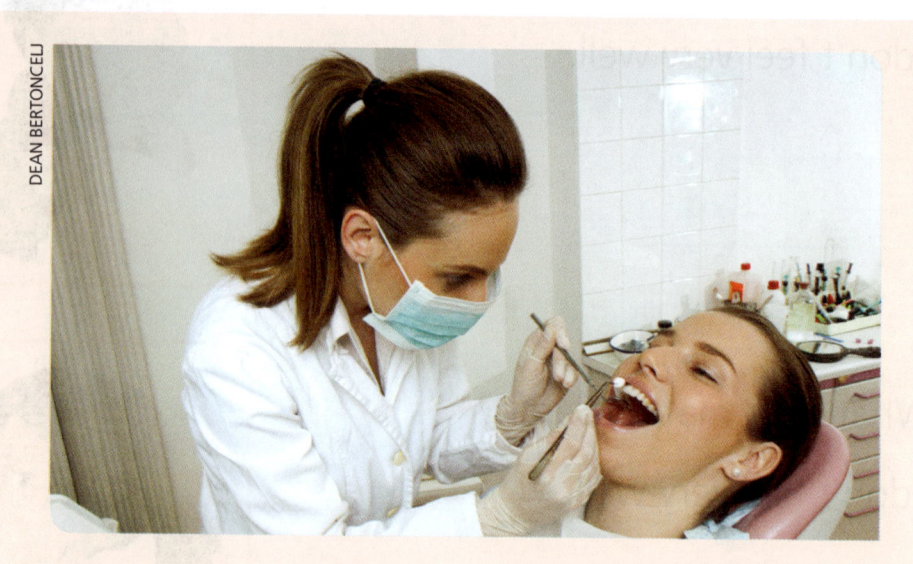

My name is Fabiane.

I'm a dentist. I take care of your teeth.

You must brush your teeth three times a day and go to a dentist every year.

Don't eat a lot of sugar, right?

6 Check the sentences as true (T) or false (F).
(Assinale se as frases são verdadeiras ou falsas.)

a) Fabiane is a dentist.

☐ T ☐ F

b) We must brush our teeth three times a day.

☐ T ☐ F

c) We must eat a lot of sugar.

☐ T ☐ F

7 Look at the pictures and find the words.
(Olhe as figuras e encontre as palavras.)

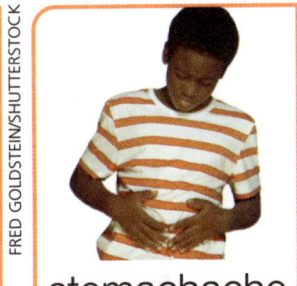

headache — sore throat — fever — earache

cold — cough — backache — stomachache

H	E	A	D	A	C	H	E	M	Y	C	O	L	D	B
A	B	E	K	A	K	S	C	L	A	E	H	N	F	G
F	E	V	E	R	R	J	D	B	G	M	M	D	O	S
C	B	J	I	D	C	Z	H	F	X	G	I	N	F	O
T	H	F	S	T	O	M	A	C	H	A	C	H	E	R
I	Q	D	C	C	E	U	U	V	L	P	H	J	Q	E
G	H	C	O	U	G	H	T	K	V	Q	I	V	U	T
P	E	I	M	R	H	S	J	K	X	R	U	J	R	H
F	L	G	N	U	X	E	A	R	A	C	H	E	S	R
D	O	B	V	F	L	T	E	N	K	T	S	A	T	O
B	A	C	K	A	C	H	E	M	D	L	Z	O	B	A
M	C	N	S	A	O	Z	Q	B	R	C	C	X	V	T

77

8 Let's write.
(Vamos escrever.)

What's wrong? (Qual é o problema?/O que há de errado?)	**Maybe you should...** (Talvez você devesse...)
• I have a fever. (Estou com febre.)	• ...see a doctor. (...ir ao médico.)
• I have a headache. (Estou com dor de cabeça.)	• ...go to the dentist. (...ir ao dentista.)
• I have a toothache. (Estou com dor de dente.)	• ...take a shower. (...tomar um banho.)
• I have a stomachache. (Estou com dor de estômago.)	• ...go to bed. (...ir para a cama.)
• I have a cold. (Estou resfriado.)	• ...take an aspirin. (...tomar uma aspirina.)
• I have a sore throat. (Estou com dor de garganta.)	• ...drink a cup of tea. (...tomar uma xícara de chá.)
• I have a cough. (Estou com tosse.)	• ...go to a hospital. (...ir para um hospital.)
• I have an earache. (Estou com dor de ouvido.)	• ...take some syrup. (...tomar um xarope.)

Example:
— I have a headache.
— You should take an aspirin.

a) She has a _____. (cold)

She should _____.

b) I have a _____. (fever)

You should _____.

c) He has a _____. (stomachache)

He should _____.

d) I have a _____. (toothache)

You should _____.

e) We have _____. (sore throat)

You should _____.

f) I have a _____. (cough)

You should _____.

g) They have _____. (earache)

They should _____.

9 Listen and match.
(Escute e ligue.)

| George | Susan | Ann | Robert |
| Suzy | Allan | Michael | Julia |

headache

earache

stomachache

sore throat

fever

cold

cough

toothache

81

LESSON 8

WHAT DID EVERYBODY DO LAST WEEKEND?

(O que todo mundo fez no último fim de semana?)

Listen and read.
(Escute e leia.)

We **went** to the movies.

They **played** soccer.

I **stayed** at home.

She **went** to the club.

I **visited** some friends.

We **had** a barbecue.

They **ate** pizza.

Read the messages.
(Leia as mensagens.)

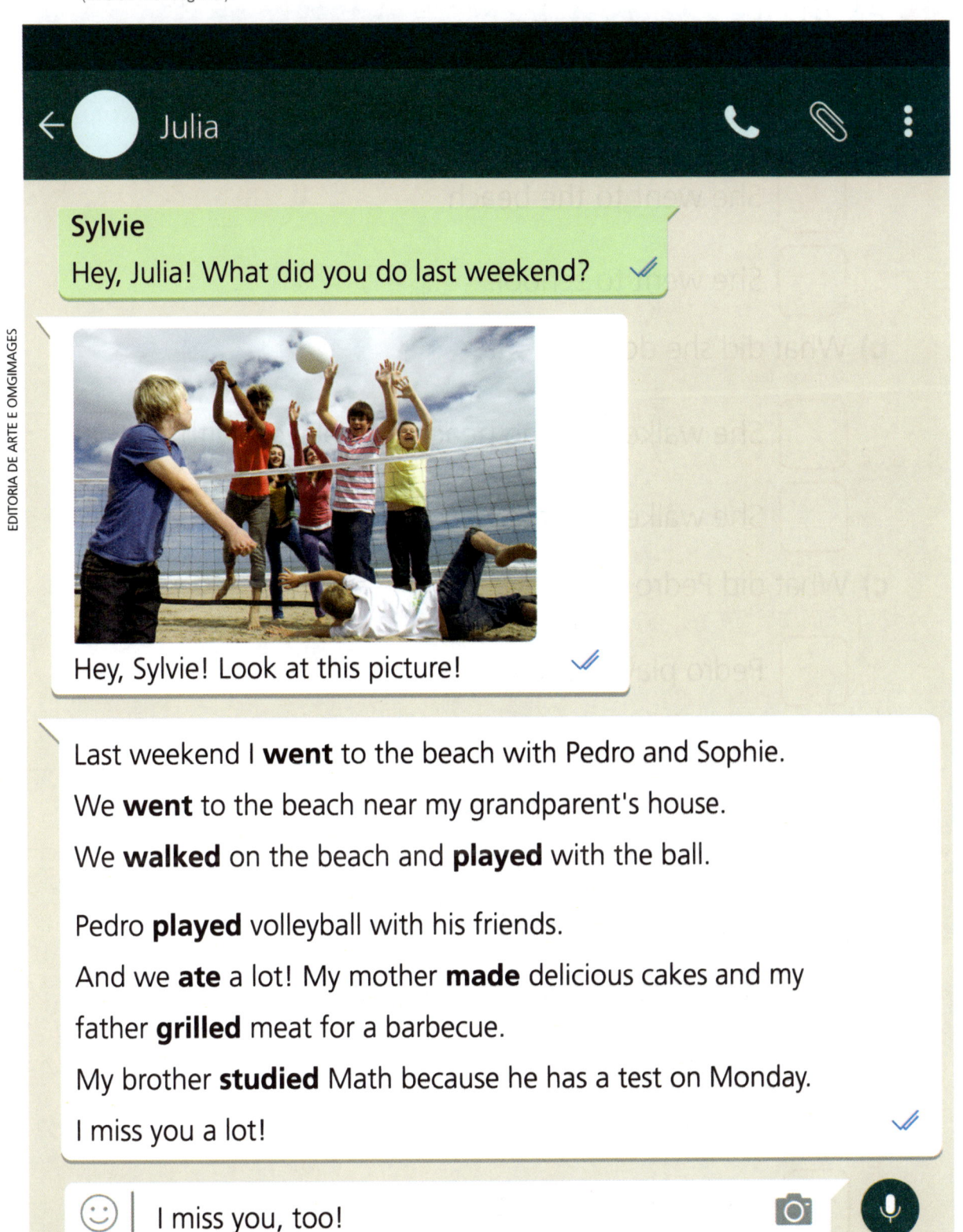

Julia

Sylvie
Hey, Julia! What did you do last weekend?

Hey, Sylvie! Look at this picture!

Last weekend I **went** to the beach with Pedro and Sophie.

We **went** to the beach near my grandparent's house.

We **walked** on the beach and **played** with the ball.

Pedro **played** volleyball with his friends.

And we **ate** a lot! My mother **made** delicious cakes and my father **grilled** meat for a barbecue.

My brother **studied** Math because he has a test on Monday.

I miss you a lot!

I miss you, too!

ACTIVITIES

1 **Choose the correct answers.**
(Escolha as respostas corretas.)

a) Where did Julia go last weekend?
(Onde Júlia esteve no fim de semana passado?)

☐ She went to the beach.

☐ She went to school.

b) What did she do?
(O que ela fez?)

☐ She walked on the beach and played with the ball.

☐ She walked on the beach and played soccer.

c) What did Pedro do?
(O que Pedro fez?)

☐ Pedro played soccer.

☐ Pedro played volleyball.

d) Who grilled for a barbecue?
(Quem fez o churrasco?)

☐ Her father made the cakes.

☐ Her father grilled for a barbecue.

e) Who has a test?

☐ Her brother has a test.

☐ Her sister has a test.

2 Find the past tense of the following verbs.
(Encontre o passado dos seguintes verbos.)

| go | visit | stay | see |
| eat | play | grill | help |

W	E	N	T	A	J	H	E	L	P	E	D	A	S
K	H	G	F	B	I	D	J	X	B	Q	V	X	A
P	P	I	T	A	T	E	D	Z	V	Y	Z	A	W
L	V	C	U	H	C	E	C	Y	U	K	B	L	A
A	Y	F	E	B	W	P	V	I	S	I	T	E	D
Y	S	D	G	L	M	O	Q	E	D	R	S	M	T
E	G	R	H	K	N	P	F	J	C	D	M	N	O
D	F	Q	I	D	O	S	T	A	Y	E	D	I	H
Z	A	G	R	I	L	L	E	D	K	L	P	T	U

Put the verbs found in the right position.
(Coloque os verbos encontrados na posição correta.)

Go _____

Play _____

Eat _____

Stay _____

Visit _____

Grill _____

See _____

Help _____

85

LET'S SEE SOME VERBS IN THE PAST
(Vamos ver alguns verbos no passado)

simple present	simple past	translation
brush	brushed	escovar
drink	drank	beber
eat	ate	comer
feel	felt	sentir
go	went	ir
grill	grilled	grelhar
have	had	ter
help	helped	ajudar
like	liked	gostar
listen	listened	ouvir
look	looked	olhar
make	made	fazer
play	played	jogar, tocar
see	saw	ver
study	studied	estudar
take	took	tomar, pegar
travel	traveled	viajar
visit	visited	visitar
write	wrote	escrever

3 Now, write sentences about your last weekend.
(Agora escreva frases sobre o seu último fim de semana).

> went to the beach
> (fui à praia)
> studied
> (estudei)
>
> played soccer
> (joguei futebol)
> had chocolate cake
> (comi bolo de chocolate)

Last weekend, I _____

_____

_____ .

Attention!
(Atenção!)

- last weekend
  (fim de semana passado)
- last week
  (semana passada)
- last month
  (mês passado)
- yesterday
  (ontem)
- last night
  (ontem à noite)

4 Listen and complete.
(Escute e complete).

Last november, I _____ my grandparents in Angra dos Reis. I _____ on holidays with my parents. I _____ with my cousins on the beach. We _____ volleyball and had a barbecue with all my family. I _____ it a lot!

87

5 Let's play! Go to page 125.
(Vamos brincar! Vá para a página 125.)

6 Write these sentences in the past. Use the words in the following box.
(Escreva estas frases no passado. Use as palavras do boxe a seguir.)

> Example:
> Nancy levantou cedo.
> Nancy **woke up early**.

> ... had breakfast.
> ... did some exercise.
> ... went to the park.
> ... brushed her teeth.
> ... washed her face.

a) Ela escovou os dentes.

She _____.

b) Ela lavou o rosto.

She _____.

c) Ela tomou café da manhã.

She _____.

d) Nancy fez exercícios.

Nancy _____.

e) Ela foi ao parque.

She _____.

7 Go to page 127. Glue the pictures and write the sentences in the past.
(Vá para a página 127. Cole as figuras e escreva as frases no passado.)

8 Let's write.
(Vamos escrever.)

> **Example:**
> What did you do last weekend?
> (O que você fez no fim de semana passado?)
>
> I **had** a party. **(have)**
> (Dei uma festa.)

a) What did you do last weekend?

_____. (study English)

b) What did she do yesterday?

_____. (play soccer)

c) What did he do last night?

_____. (see a movie)

d) What did they do last morning?

_____. (watch TV)

e) What did you do last week?

_____. (go to school)

f) What did your mother do last night?

_____. (read a book)

g) What did you do last Sunday?

_____. (go to the zoo)

9 Interview a friend and write the answers.
(Entreviste um/a amigo/a e escreva as respostas.)

played basketball. visited my grandparents.
watched TV. went to school.
traveled to the beach. studied for a test.

Example:
What did you do last weekend?
I **studied** for a test.

a) What did you do yesterday?
_____
_____

b) What did you do last night?
_____
_____

c) What did you do last weekend?
_____
_____

d) What did you do last week?
_____
_____

e) What did you do yesterday morning?
_____
_____

REVIEW
(Revisão)

I can talk about activities in the past. (Eu sei conversar sobre fatos que aconteceram no passado.)		
• last week	• last weekend	• last month

1 Answer.
(Responda.)

a) What did your father do last weekend?

He _____.

b) What did your friend do last weekend?

He/She _____.

I learned some verbs and their past tenses.
(Eu aprendi alguns verbos e sua forma no passado.)

2 Let's put them into the past tense.
(Vamos colocá-los no passado.)

a) study _____   f) make _____

b) go _____   g) have _____

c) visit _____   h) play _____

d) eat _____   i) see _____

e) drink _____   j) take _____

3 Tell everything you did yesterday.
(Conte tudo o que você fez ontem.)

_____

_____

_____

_____

_____

_____

4 Write the following sentences in the simple past.
(Escreva as seguintes frases no *simple past*.)

a) He studies English.

_____

b) I play volleyball at school.

_____

c) They stay at home.

_____

d) We watch TV.

_____

e) He helps his mother a lot.

_____

f) It is a very beautiful cat.

_____

GLOSSARY
(Glossário)

A

a lot of: muito(a), bastante
apartment: apartamento
apple: maçã
apple pie: torta de maçã

B

backache: dor nas costas
bad: mau, má
banana: banana
bank: banco
barbecue: churrasco
beach: praia
bean: feijão
beautiful: lindo(a)
bedroom: quarto
belt: cinto
big: grande
bikini: biquíni
blouse: blusa
bookstore: livraria
boots: botas
box: caixa
bracelet: pulseira
bread: pão
breakfast: café da manhã
broccoli: brócolis
brush: escova, escovar
butter: manteiga

C

cake: bolo
cap: boné
carrot: cenoura
carton: embalagem longa vida
cauliflower: couve-flor
cheap: barato(a)
chicken: frango
chocolate cake: bolo de chocolate
choose: escolher
Christmas: Natal
clothes: roupas
coffee: café
coffee shop: cafeteria, café
cold: resfriado
comfortable: cômodo, confortável
corn flakes: flocos de milho
cup: xícara
cycling: ciclismo

D

dentist: dentista
dessert: sobremesa
dinner: jantar
dress: vestido
drink: bebida
drugstore: farmácia

E

earache: dor de ouvido
earrings: brincos
eat: comer

F

factory: fábrica
fall: outono
family: família
fever: febre
find: encontrar, achar
fish: peixe
food: comida
French fries: batatas fritas
fresh: fresco(a)
fridge: geladeira
fruit: fruta, frutas
fruit salad: salada de frutas

G

go: ir
good: bom, boa
grill: grelhar
grilled: grelhado(a) / grelhou

H

hamburger: hambúrguer
happy: feliz
headache: dor de cabeça
house: casa

I

interview: entrevista

J

jacket: jaqueta
jam: geleia
juice: suco

L

large: grande
lemon: limão
lettuce: alface
list: lista
live: viver, morar
lunch: almoço

M

mall: *shopping center*
margarine: margarina
mayonnaise: maionese
medium: médio(a)
milk: leite
movie theater: cinema
movies: cinema

N

necklace: colar
need: precisar
new: novo(a)
now: agora
number(s): número(s)

O

old: velho(a)
onion: cebola
orange: laranja
order: pedido

95

P

package: pacote
party: festa
pasta: massas
pear: pera
pie: torta
plate: prato
play: jogar, tocar, brincar
post office: correio
potato(es): batata(s)

R

ready: pronto(a)
restaurant: restaurante
rice: arroz
rice and beans: arroz e feijão

S

salad: salada
sandals: sandália
scarf: cachecol
school: escola
sentence: frase, sentença
size: tamanho
small: pequeno(a)
soccer: futebol
socks: meias
soda: refrigerante
sorethroat: dor de garganta
soup: sopa
spinach: espinafre
sport: esporte
spring: primavera
steak: bife
stomachache: dor de estômago
summer: verão
supermarket: supermercado
sweater: blusa de frio
swim: nadar

T

table: mesa
tea: chá
tennis: tênis (esporte)
tennis shoes: tênis
tomato(es): tomate(s)
travel: viajar
T-shirt: camiseta

V

vacation: férias
vegetables: legumes
volleyball: vôlei

W

weekend: fim de semana
winter: inverno
wrong: errado(a)

Coleção

Eu gosto m@is

ALMANAQUE

ARCHITECT

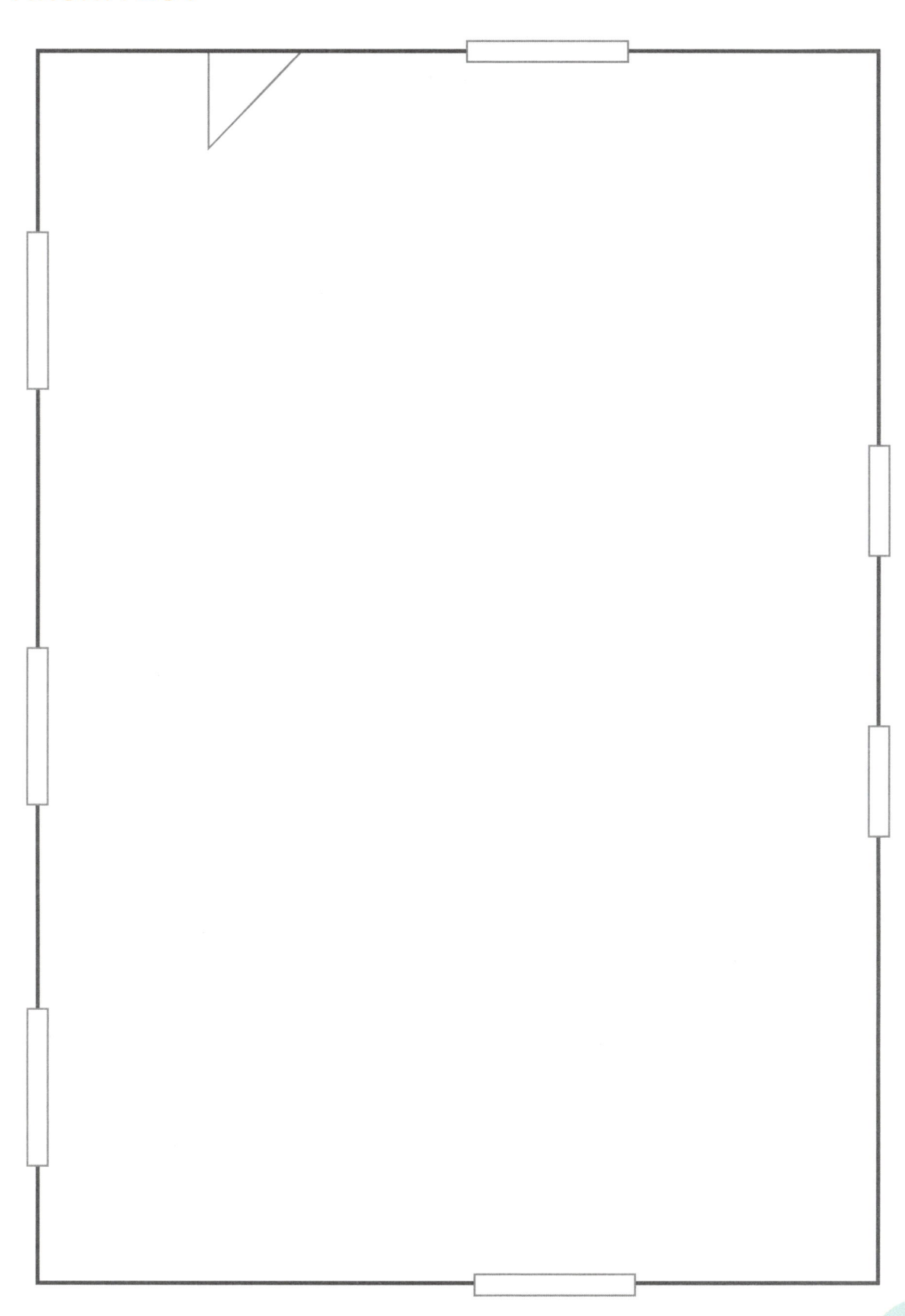

COMPLEMENTARY ACTIVITIES

MEMORY GAME

Cut
(Cortar)

COMPLEMENTARY ACTIVITIES

	**apples** (maçãs)		**milk** (leite)
bread (pães)		**bananas** (bananas)	
	**rice** (arroz)		
broccoli (brócolis)		**lemons** (limões)	**lettuce** (alface)
onions (cebolas)		**pears** (peras)	

101

Parte integrante da Coleção Eu Gosto M@is – Língua Inglesa 3º ano – IBEP.

FOOD DOMINO

Cut
(Cortar)

COMPLEMENTARY ACTIVITIES

LEMON	LEMON	LEMON	LEMON	BANANA	CARROT	CARROT
ORANGE	CARROT	BANANA	LEMON	ORANGE	BANANA	CARROT
LEMON	CARROT	CARROT	BANANA	ORANGE	ORANGE	ORANGE
APPLE	APPLE	ORANGE	BANANA	LETTUCE	APPLE	ORANGE
LEMON	CARROT	BANANA	BANANA	LETTUCE	LETTUCE	APPLE
LETTUCE	LETTUCE	LETTUCE	APPLE	LETTUCE	APPLE	APPLE
LEMON	CARROT	BANANA	ORANGE	LETTUCE	APPLE	POTATO
POTATO	POTATO	POTATO	POTATO	POTATO	POTATO	POTATO

103

Parte integrante da Coleção Eu Gosto M@is – Língua Inglesa 3º ano – IBEP.

MATCH THE NUMBERS

☐ twelve		19 ☐	
☐ seventeen		11 ☐	
☐ eighteen		16 ☐	
☐ thirty-two		20 ☐	
☐ fourteen		36 ☐	
☐ forty-one		47 ☐	
☐ fifty		15 ☐	
☐ ten		13 ☐	

MATCH THE NUMBERS (2)

✂ Cut
(Cortar)

14	thirty-six
17	forty-seven
10	fifteen
50	twenty
12	nineteen
32	eleven
41	thirteen
18	sixteen

BINGO

✂ Cut
(Cortar)

THERE IS / THERE ARE

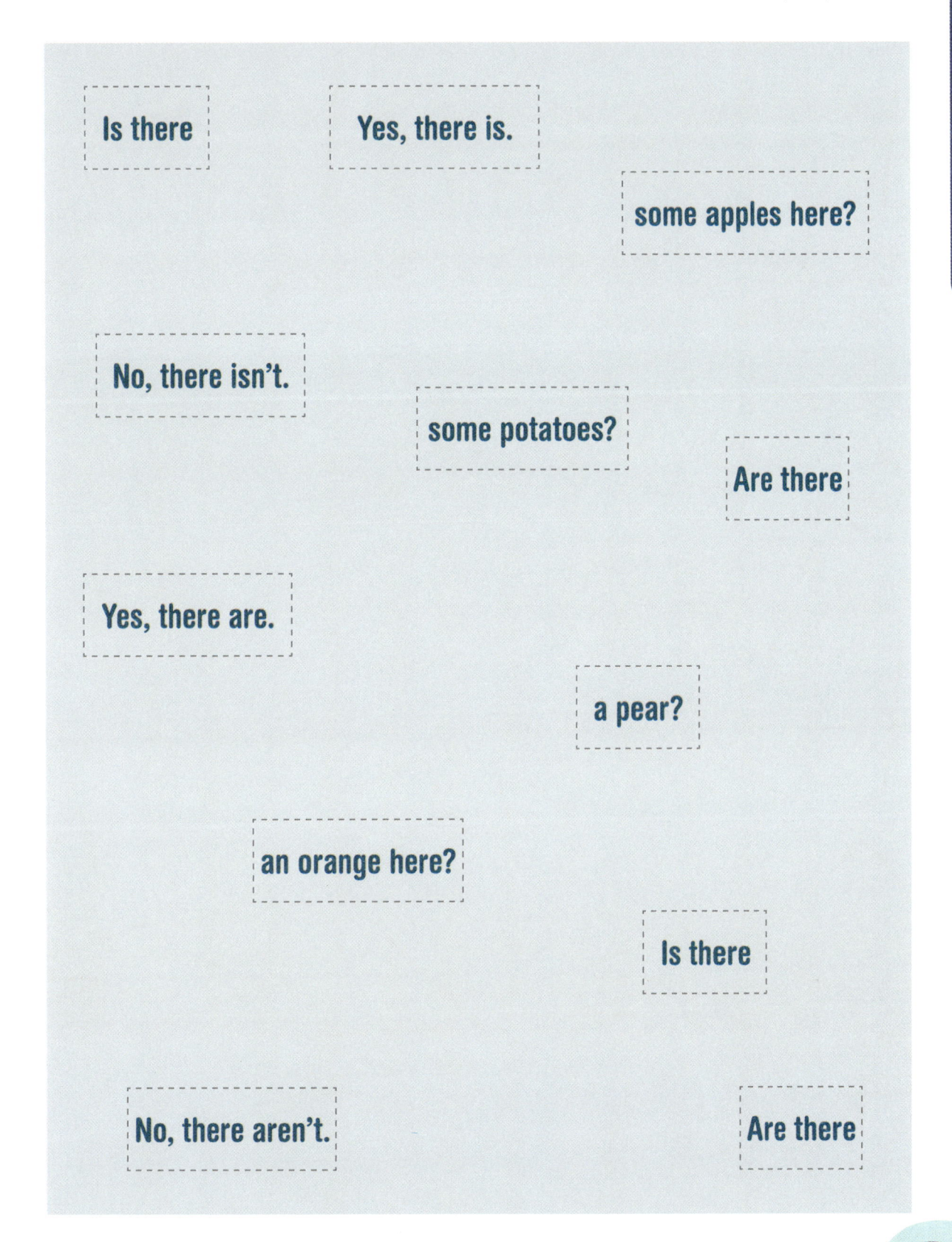

✂ Cut
(Cortar)

COMPLEMENTARY ACTIVITIES

Is there

Yes, there is.

some apples here?

No, there isn't.

some potatoes?

Are there

Yes, there are.

a pear?

an orange here?

Is there

No, there aren't.

Are there

111

Parte integrante da Coleção Eu Gosto M@is – Língua Inglesa 3º ano – IBEP.

COMPLEMENTARY ACTIVITIES

113

DAILY ACTIVITIES

	Morning	Afternoon	Evening
Monday			
Tuesday			
Wednesday			
Thursday			
Friday			
Saturday			
Sunday			

COMPLEMENTARY ACTIVITIES

Parte integrante da Coleção Eu Gosto M@is – Língua Inglesa 3º ano – IBEP.

DAILY ACTIVITIES (2)

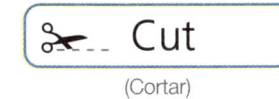

✂ Cut
(Cortar)

COMPLEMENTARY ACTIVITIES

English class	Play videogames	Watch TV
Go to the library	Go to school	Do my homework
Watch TV	Go to school	Do my homework
Play with my friends	Go to school	Do my homework
Go to the shopping center	Go to school	Do my homework
Play volleyball	Go to school	Do my homework
Play with my friends	Play videogames	Play soccer
Watch TV	Play soccer	Go to a restaurant

Parte integrante da Coleção Eu Gosto M@is – Língua Inglesa 3º ano – IBEP.

PIECE OF CLOTHING

✂ Cut
(Cortar)

COMPLEMENTARY ACTIVITIES

MAKE YOUR MENU

Cut
(Cortar)

COMPLEMENTARY ACTIVITIES

KIDS MENU

FOOD

_____ R$ _____
_____ R$ _____
_____ R$ _____
_____ R$ _____
_____ R$ _____
_____ R$ _____
_____ R$ _____

DRINK

_____ R$ _____
_____ R$ _____
_____ R$ _____

DESSERT

_____ R$ _____
_____ R$ _____
_____ R$ _____
_____ R$ _____

Parte integrante da Coleção Eu Gosto M@is – Língua Inglesa 3º ano – IBEP.

Menu

	Hamburger	R$ 18,00
	Cheeseburger	R$ 21,00
	French fries (Batatas fritas)	R$ 14,00
	Hot dog (Cachorro-quente)	R$ 11,00
	Grilled chicken (Frango grelhado)	R$ 25,00
	Potato salad (Salada de batatas)	R$ 20,00
	Fish (Peixe)	R$ 30,00
	Vegetables (Legumes)	R$ 18,00
	Salad (Salada)	R$ 22,00
	Rice and beans (Arroz e feijão)	R$ 14,00
	Soup (Sopa)	R$ 14,00
	Pasta (Macarrão)	R$ 20,00

Desserts

Ice cream (Sorvete)		R$ 7,25
Chocolate cake (Bolo de chocolate)		R$ 7,50
Banana pie (Torta de banana)		R$ 7,50
Fruit salad (Salada de frutas)		R$ 8,25

Drinks

Water (Água)		R$ 3,50
Orange juice (Suco de laranja)		R$ 8,00
Soda (Refrigerante)		R$ 4,50

COMPLEMENTARY ACTIVITIES

FOTOGRAFIAS: SHUTTERSTOCK

Cut (Cortar)

Parte integrante da Coleção Eu Gosto M@is – Língua Inglesa 3º ano – IBEP.

Cut
(Cortar)

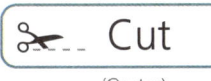

COMPLEMENTARY ACTIVITIES

drink	had
eat	played
go	ate
have	visited
make	took
play	drank
see	made
study	went
take	studied
visit	saw

125

Parte integrante da Coleção Eu Gosto M@is – Língua Inglesa 3º ano – IBEP.

✂ Cut
(Cortar)

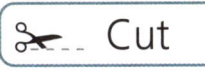

COMPLEMENTARY ACTIVITIES

ILUSTRAÇÕES: LAVINIA DANIELA TRIFAN POP

127
Parte integrante da Coleção Eu Gosto M@is – Língua Inglesa 3º ano – IBEP.